D1302865

The Films
of
Mary Pickford

The Films

of

Mary Pickford

RAYMOND LEE

CASTLE BOOKS ★ NEW YORK

This Edition Published by Arrangement
with A. S. Barnes & Co., Inc.

Printed in the United States of America

Contents

Acknowledgments

Academy of Motion Picture Arts & Sciences
EDWARD WAGENKNECHT
GENE RINGGOLD
B. C. VAN HECHT
LARRY EDMUNDS BOOKSHOP
THE SCROUNGERS MOVIE MEMORABILIA SHOP
ALPHA BOOKS, BETTY VASIN
MANUEL WELTMAN
JOHN HAMPTON

Introduction

I have often said that I do not believe anybody can understand America in the years during and after the First World War who does not understand the vogue of Mary Pickford. She was the undisputed Queen of the Movies for many years, a national ideal who set the standard by which others were judged. No other woman ever had such a career in pictures or ever can have. Garbo has been a cult but what she did to the box office was insignificant compared to what Mary had done there; she was too foreign and too sophisticated to possess our hearts as Mary did, and in her time the tendencies which have since quite destroyed the film as a popular art were already beginning to make themselves felt. Marilyn *was* a great box office performer, and she was deeply loved too, but she was loved differently than Mary.

I have tried, though I think with indifferent success, to analyze Mary's appeal in *The Movies in the Age of Innocence;* how can you ever tell anybody why you care for somebody else? and have not observers been asking since time immemorial what *he* can possibly see in *her* or *she* in *him*? "America's Sweetheart" had a love affair with a whole nation and a whole generation; it was a curiously chaste love affair, but there was nothing cold or prissy or saccharine about it. You did not need to explain your feelings at the time, for nine out of every ten people you met shared them with you. If you who read do not now understand this because you have not had the good fortune to see her films, I am sorry for you, and I am trying to do my best for you, but this will be no equivalent to what you would have done for yourself if you had lived in better times.

9

I think the earliest Pickford film I recall is *Lena and the Geese,* though I am sure I must have seen her even before that. I remember one of her almost completely forgotten Majestics, *Little Red Riding Hood,* and Imp's *In the Sultan's Garden* spread out all the glories of Orientalism before my childishly enraptured eyes. Yet I must confess I had no idea, during the pre-feature era, that she was destined to soar beyond the three Florences (Lawrence, Turner, and LaBadie), Blanche Sweet, Gene Gauntier, Alice Joyce, Gwendolen Pates, and all the other ladies I admired. Nowadays many actresses look like something that has been delivered by auto truck, but that was a generation rich in feminine charm.

In 1915 we moved to Oak Park, and one night I went to the Oak Park Theater to see Mary Pickford in the first "feature" in which I had encountered her, *Fanchon the Cricket.* I never missed another Pickford film, and though I had a good deal of catching-up to do, I ran all over Chicago and accomplished it.

I soon learned, however, that not missing a Pickford film did not mean seeing it once; it meant seeing it as many times as it came your way. Films did not then have the long runs they have today, for many "fans" went to the "movies" every night, and they demanded frequent changes of bill. I saw Mary in *Pollyanna* more than twenty times, and I should have duplicated that record on many of the others if I had had the chance.

My correspondence with Miss Pickford began early, and she soon sent me a beautiful sepia photograph of herself with a personal inscription. When she came east on her honeymoon with Douglas Fairbanks, I met her, by appointment, at the Blackstone Hotel. When I myself was married, my bride and I visited her in California, and when our first child was born, she became his godmother at her own suggestion (she had ordered a boy). We have not met often, for we live far apart, I am allergic to travel, and her travels do not often bring her my way. But when I see a Pickford film today, she still affects me as she did so long ago. My only quarrel with her is that she has not so far released her films to the 8 mm. distributors, so that I can see them as often as I see the great Griffith films.

I have said that my generation's love affair with Mary Pickford was chaste, but I would not have you think that I mean there was something lacking in it. James Card, of George Eastman House, has written that there was something heavenly about Mary Pickford. So there was, and when a film required her to take on a Madonna-like aspect, she always achieved it with ease. But she had a much wider range than most people have given her credit for. No other adult has ever been able to play children on the screen as she did it, and her adolescent roles were convincingly real, full of mischief, though not of spite. In *Stella Maris* she proved herself a fine character actress, and *Suds* is as good as the best of Keaton or Sennett. Look at an Imp or early Biograph, and you will find that she was already a disciplined actress of dignity and restraint while her colleagues were still under the impression that the best acting involved breaking up the furniture. It is true, of course, that some people do not like heaven, which is probably the reason so many of them opt for hell. But for us of the generation that was closest to her, Mary's heaven embraced all we needed of human warmth and sympathy, and we were abundantly contented in it.

EDWARD WAGENKNECHT

The Films
of
Mary Pickford

Queen of the Screen

On a Spring morning in 1909, in New York City, a sixteen-year-old girl, looking like twelve, walked into the reception room of the Biograph Studios, shook her long, golden curls at the secretary behind the desk and asked to see David Wark Griffith.

As she remembered the fateful moment:

"I did not think much of the movies at that time. In fact, people on the legitimate stage considered it a disgrace to work in pictures. But my mother had asked me to try and see Mr. Griffith. Although I demurred, she insisted, and of course I could not disobey.

"But I took the precaution to route my trip so that I could make five cents do the work of ten. Those were the times when five cents was always doing the work of ten.

"Instead of taking a street car from where we lived to the studio, I walked the ten blocks, took the car on Fourteenth and asked for a transfer. The old Biograph was between Broadway and Fifth Avenue. Thus, when I had satisfied mother, I could walk back to Broadway and use my transfer to ride to Times Square and the theatrical district where the booking offices were located.

"I felt certain that in the end it would be necessary to visit them to obtain another engagement, which at that moment I needed very badly . . . "

The secretary replied that Mr. Griffith was seeing no one. As the little girl turned to leave, a man crossing the foyer almost bumped into her. He stopped short, stared down at her, suddenly touched one of her curls.

"Are you an actress?"

"I most certainly am."

"What, if any, experience have you had?"

"Only ten years in the theatre, sir, and two of them with Mr. David Belasco."

A twinkle flashed in his eye as he ran a finger down his long nose.

"You're too little and too fat, but I think I'll give you a chance. My name is Griffith. We'll pay you five dollars a day."

The golden curls shook vigorously.

"I said I was a Belasco actress, Mr. Griffith, and I must have ten!"

A hearty laugh filled the foyer.

"Agreed! Five dollars for today's test and ten for tomorrow's work day. But keep it to yourself. No one is paid that much, and there will be a riot if it leaks out."

As the Father of Films reached for the little girl's hand, she dropped the street car transfer on the marble floor and followed him up the old staircase. Gladys Smith had taken her first steps to becoming Mary Pickford, morning star of the silent screen.

Throughout their historic association, little Mary was constantly asking Griffith for more money. Much of her demands were based on not just a little prevarication.

One morning she cornered D. W. with a face quite red from what looked like embarrassment.

"Mr. Griffith, I've never been so embarrassed in my life! This morning on the subway my brother Jack threatened to tell everyone I was the 'Biograph Girl' if I didn't give him fifteen cents."

"Well, what's wrong with that? You are now."

As though she hadn't heard him, she continued her pleading:

"I knew he would do it so I gave him the money. So now I must have a ten dollar raise."

"To pay off brother Jack's blackmail?"

The golden curls shook like a windmill.

"Mr. Griffith, that's not the proper word to use regarding my brother's efforts to get money from me. Besides, he was just a part of it."

"Pickford" (he never called her Mary) "are you any better an actress this week than you were last?"

She again shook her curls and continued:

"Mr. Griffith, two people *did* recognize me as the 'Biograph Girl.' Two strangers spoke to me. If I am going to be embarrassed in public that way I must have more money."

Griffith, guffawing, took out his watch.

"Five minutes for a better reason."

16

Nothing but the sound of the great director's watch ticking away could be heard until Griffith, smiling, broke the silence and sighed:

"You know, Pickford, I'd give my whole salary if just *one* person recognized me in the subway!"

For 23 years and in more than 125 short features and 52 full length films, Mary Pickford ruled as queen of the screen. And many stars were born to her line of the Golden Curls.

Marguerite Clarke, Mary Miles Minter, Mildred Harris—to name a few. All tried to follow in Mary's footsteps but none equaled her.

As one of her many directors, Cecil B. DeMille, wrote:

"Somewhere, sometime, a phrase was born: 'America's Sweetheart.'

"Thousands of such phrases are born daily in Hollywood. Most of them, mercifully, die young.

"About once in a generation such a phrase lives, because it is more than a phrase: it is a fact.

"I do not know who first called Mary Pickford 'America's Sweetheart,' but, whoever he was, he put into two words the most remarkable personal achievement of its kind in the history of motion pictures.

"There have been hundreds of stars. There have been scores of fine actresses in motion pictures. There has been only one Mary Pickford . . ."[1]

America's Sweetheart . . .

From her $40 a week start with Griffith, Pickford became the most famous woman of her times and one of the world's richest. Those who dealt with her across the contract table came away believing her real heart was that of an iron-butterfly—despite dimples, golden curls, and a smile that could sweep the world into her arms.

Ben Hampton, pioneer film historian wrote:

"Although theatres, studios and exchanges in 1917-1918 represented investments of several millions of dollars, and gave employment to 100,000 people, Pickford remained the movies' most valuable asset —she was the only member of her sex who ever became the focal point of an entire industry."[2]

Adolph Zukor bore the marks of many a Pickford demand for salary increases. Zukor once offered her $10,000 a week. She dimpled, twirled a curl—and refused. He countered with a $250,000 bonus providing she would not make films for any of his competitors for five years. "I love pictures," she countered, and "I'm just a girl. I

1. Reprinted through the courtesy of Prentice-Hall.

2. Reprinted through the courtesy of Ben Hampton.

couldn't quit now." And she didn't, signing instead with First National for three features totalling $1,050,000.

Terry Ramsaye summed up the fantastic influence of the girl-woman:

"The high price of Pickford put Zukor into picture exhibition on Broadway. He wanted to set a pace for the nation and give his pictures the glamour of 'The Great White Way.'

"Players sought exaggerated salaries and gave out over-inflated reports of what they did earn. In turn competitors began to announce bigger and bigger salaries, regardless of the fact, to make their plays and players seem as important as Mary Pickford and her pictures. They started in thousands and got to millions in about two years.

"Now the public began to acquire its impression of the motion picture as an institution of unlimited wealth and glorious extravagance.

"See what Mary Did!"[3]

And what she was to do.

Married to Douglas Fairbanks, both at the peak of their careers, she asked a gathering at Wm. G. McAdoo's bungalow in Santa Barbara, California, "Why should we toil for producers who make all the profit? Why can't we be our own bosses?"

As a result of this query United Artists was born. It included Mary, Doug, Charlie Chaplin and D. W. Griffith. Western star William S. Hart had been asked to join but Zukor tempted him with a $200,000 per picture guarantee, and he went with Mr. Z.

Of this union Richard Rowland, then head of Metro Pictures Corporation, uttered the classic comment:

"So the lunatics have taken charge of the asylum."

Arthur L. Mayer and Richard Griffith comment on the lunatic proceedings that led to abundant profits:

"Most of the early gatherings of the partners were marked by levity. Doug's idea of subtle humor was to disappear under the table and terrify an honored guest by grabbing his, or preferably her, calf, or he would wire a chair so as to give some visiting VIP an unexpected shock.

"There were plenty of such visitors, particularly attorneys. So meticulous were the artists in the protection of their interests that it required 10 eminent legal lights to draw up the initial contracts.

"Mary used to listen to all of them carefully, shake her lovely curls and say: 'I disagree with you gentlemen and I will tell you why.'

3. Reprinted from *A Million and One Nights,* through the courtesy of Simon and Shuster.

18

The 'why' was invariably connected with unnecessary expenditures. She was usually right."[4]

So who knew where the two hearts of America's Mary beat.

The fans loved only one heart and they didn't care if some said it was gold-plated.

The Pickford gallery of cinema portraits is quite a surprise when one thinks of her only as "Pollyanna," "Rebecca of Sunnybrook Farm" and "Little Annie Rooney." Cinderella personified.

But dynamic characterizations show how rough and ready little Mary could be. For *Heart of the Hills* she was a night rider in the robes of the Ku Klux Klan bringing justice to a mountain community. To rescue her drunken father in *Rags* she waged a battle royal in a frontier saloon. Saving a kidnapped infant from being thrown into quicksand for *Sparrows*, Mary bested the villain with a pitchfork and then led a handful of kiddies through a nightmare swamp with alligators snapping at almost every footstep.

She won the first Oscar for the best performance by an actress in sound in 1929. She played a young southern belle who faces the birth of an illegitimate child. The picture—*Coquette*.

Many have tried and failed to define Pickford's genius.

Poet Vachel Lindsay expressed what he felt was the secret:

"Botticelli painted her portrait many centuries ago when by some necromancy she appeared to him in this phase of herself . . .

"The people are hungry for this fine and spiritual thing that Botticelli painted in the faces of his Muses and heavenly creatures. Because the Mob catch the very glimpse of it in Mary's face, they follow her night after night in the films . . ."

A review from the *New York Dramatic Mirror* for March 4, 1916, is a charming complaint:

"To analyze the acting of Mary Pickford is about as satisfactory as trying to draw a definite conclusion from a metaphysical premise. After much circumlocution, after the use of many words and the expenditure of much grey matter one is forced to the inevitable conclusion that Mary Pickford is Mary Pickford. She has a charm, a manner, an expression that is all her own. She seems to have the happy faculty of becoming for the time being the character she is portraying. At no time does one gather the impression that Mary Pickford is acting. She is the epitome of naturalness.

"But why go on? The sum and substance of it all is that Mary

4. Reprinted through the courtesy of Arthur L. Mayer.

Pickford is unique, and irrespective of the strength or weakness of any picture in which she appears, the fact that Mary Pickford appears in it makes it a good picture."

James Card sums up:

"Without the certain vision of poets, most writers now, in assessing the historic place of Mary Pickford, confine their observations to the spectacular if not particular revealing of her financial triumphs. They generally fix on her (much more so than on Chaplin) the implied opprobrium of having firmly established the star system to the detriment of the whole course of motion picture history. Such materialistic evasion fails to probe any of the reasons that Miss Pickford's films were so successful that she was able to challenge the fiscal supremacy of Charles Chaplin."

Some have said that Pickford copied Chaplin. She had chases and situations very remindful of the little tramp. What is not remembered is that Pickford was an international star commanding $2000 a week when Chaplin was still just a Mack Sennett slapsticker.

As James Card discussed this interesting comparison:

"Fairbanks and Chaplin were close friends. After Mary and Doug married in 1920, the three of them spent much of their free time at Pickfair. Together they screened their own and each other's films, digesting their results, their plans and their hopes. Mary wrote: 'the three of us became almost inseparable . . . we had become virtually one family.' It is not surprising that their film work bears both visible and intangible kinship."

Playing a child most of her reel life, how did Mary Pickford fare as a full-grown woman in real life?

At Biograph she fell in love and married her handsome Irish leading man, Owen Moore. Because her mother felt Moore was too old, she hid her marriage for months, giving birth to a guilt complex that doomed her union with the "nice guy who drank too much" almost from their "I do."

As Mary's star rose, the dashing Owen couldn't play the part of the dutiful husband. After four years of tumult and shouting they divorced but not without a touch of the melodramas in which they had starred. Moore, learning that Doug and Mary were dating, threatened to shoot Doug on sight. Mary finally talked some sense into Owen's head and the histrionics never materialized.

For two years Doug and Mary went together and when both their divorces became final they married March 28, 1920, in Los Angeles at the home of the Reverend Dr. Whitcome Brougher. This marriage remained a secret for three days.

20

From a $400,000 mansion called Pickfair, the king and queen of movies began their 14-year rule as Hollywood's happiest couple.

Pickfair was the grandiose mecca for the famous and the wealthy of every land and an invitation to this fabled mansion was as prized as one from the White House or the Royal Palace of London.

In 1934 Fairbanks was caught up in a London social whirl where he met and became infatuated with Lady Ashley. The Lady's husband named filmland's most famous athletic star as corespondent in a divorce action.

"America's Sweethearts" were parted by divorce in January of 1935.

Was Mary Pickford always to pay a price beyond even her magical touch?

During the production of *My Best Girl* costarring handsome Buddy Rogers (who first scored in "Wings," the World War I drama which won the initial silent movie Oscar) love again blossomed.

Two years later little Mary tied the nuptial knot again and at last she found a measure of the happiness so elusive to movie celebrities.

Some years ago she sat for an unusual keyboard portrait by the late blind pianist, Alec Templeton, who composed his musical impression of her.

As he played he spoke:

"That note, Miss Pickford, is your purposeful attitude towards life and your career. It also expresses your readiness and determination to face a situation squarely.

"That note is the driving force, the high C of your being—the need for action, the refusal to stand still. That suspended note represents your abhorrence of finality . . ."

And looking back . . . the early death of her brother Jack, a star in his own right . . . the loss of her mother and sister Lottie . . . the broken marriages. . . it seems most fitting that Mary Pickford's high C has always stood for courage . . . courage in the face of all odds. . . .

Her Portraits

Mary Pickford as a real little girl.

24

Mary Pickford

26

Portrait for Godfrey Philips cigarette cards.

Portrait by Hartsook.

29

30

Portrait by Hartsook.

Portrait by Baron de Meyer (1923).

Postal card portrait.

Mary Pickford in Rosita.

Rare study of Pickford with straight hair.

Mary and King.

36

Mary as Dorothy Vernon of Haddon Hall.

Sincerely Mary Pickford.

39

Portrait by Edward Steichen (1927).

40

41

42

Mary Pickford

Mary Pickford #28

48

Mary Pickford
33-584-P

50

Behind the Scenes

The Imp Company studio group. Pickford in center.

Julian Eltinge (famed female impersonator), Theodore Roberts, William S. Hart, Douglas Fairbanks, and Mary Pickford in War Relief, *a propaganda picture of 1917.*

"Maria," Mary's first stand-in and first of her kind (1919).

54

Douglas Fairbanks, Mary Pickford, William Randolph Hearst, Charlie Chaplin, and Raquel Meller at Hearst costume party.

A scene rehearsal for Daddy Long Legs, *1919. Here with Mary Pickford are Marshall Neilan, Charles Rosher, and Henry Crunjager.*

55

*Mary Pickford and brother Jack chat over lunch with director William Beaudine,
backed up by 1922 Rolls Royce.*

Mary has her famous curls cut.

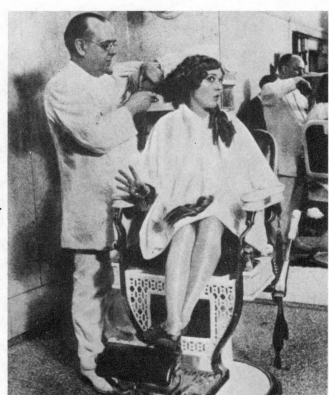

56

Mary Pickford gives director Bill Beaudine her idea of the Charleston between scenes while filming Sparrows.

Mary on set with star Laura LaPlante and visitors.

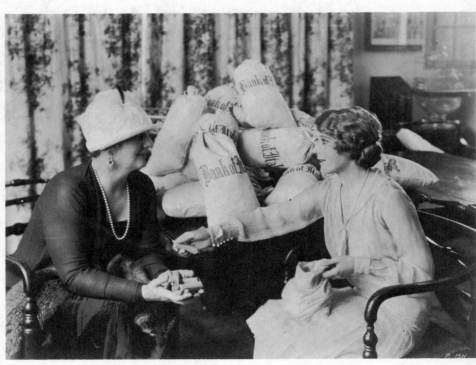

Mary Pickford pays $25,000 worth of nickels and dimes to author Kathleen Norris for the five- and ten-cent story, My Best Girl, *which Mrs. Norris wrote and which Miss Pickford produced as her new United Artist's photoplay.*

Mary Pickford won an Oscar for her performance in Coquette *in 1929.*

Mary entertaining on United Artist's lot with Charlie, Doug, and her mother.

Douglas Fairbanks, Mary Pickford, Charlie Chaplin, and D. W. Griffith on United Artists lot.

Mary shaking hand with Lupe Velez as she greets friends outside her studio bungalow.

Mary's brother Jack.

Mary Pickford and Lillian Gish.

Sam Goldwyn (left) and Jesse Lasky (right), cofounders of Paramount, shield Mary Pickford from liquid sunshine.

Mary Pickford pauses just before sailing for London. Before the ship left she said she would marry Charles (Buddy) Rogers in the United States (1937).

Mary Pickford nails a card telling of the forthcoming Pickfair China Aid benefit festival to the side of her famed home, Pickfair. Many glamor girls helped to make the event a success. The funds went to aid the Chinese war orphans and to help rebuild the bombed Chinese Orthopedic Hospital in Kweiyang, China.

Mary Pickford takes the witness stand in Superior Court to testify concerning a financial transaction in which the motion picture producing company, which she headed, was assertedly bilked of $25,000 (1934).

Mary Pickford aboard the Queen Mary, following a trip to Europe (1937).

Mary Pickford and Buddy Rogers at theatre.

Mary visiting a set.

Associated Press Photo
MARY PICKFORD, 1940

Mary Pickford knits for soldiers again. Turning back the pages of time to the days when she knitted sweaters for soldiers of the American Expeditionary Forces in 1917, Mary once again gives her time to the American Red Cross. Here she is knitting sweaters for refugees in England and on the Continent (1940).

Mary Pickford stepped off Union Pacific streamliner from the East with a brand new hat.

Summoned to Chicago by the illness of a close family friend, Mary leaves by TWA Stratoliner.

"America's sweetheart" boarding the then-new Boeing 247.

Wearing a striking hat with veil, Mary greets the press with a smile during a reception at the Savoy Hotel in London, March 27, 1946.

Mary Pickford, defendant in a suit for $1,653,750 in damages brought by director Gregory La Cava, takes the stand in Los Angeles Superior Court to testify in trial of the suit. La Cava charged breach of contract. (1947).

Movie producers, old and new. Jane Russell (right) was signed as actress-producer by United Artists on the eve of its 35th anniversary. Mary Pickford (left), one of the founders and still co-owner of the company, was the first actress-producer on the roster (March 21, 1954).

Mary Pickford takes fighting stance in describing her plans for court fight and auction bid for the Samuel Goldwyn Studios property (March 1955).

Mary enters church for the funeral of a friend (December 1955).

Even at 67 Mary still has the same familiar smile (1961).

Her Films

AT AMERICAN BIOGRAPH
Pickford made 85 one reel films directed by D. W. Griffith and photographed by G. W. Bitzer.

Titles Available—

1909: THE VIOLIN MAKER OF CREMONA—
CAST: David Miles.

THEY WOULD ELOPE—
CAST: Billy Quirk.

THE HESSIAN RENEGADES—
CAST: Billy Quirk.

IN OLD KENTUCKY—
CAST: Henry B. Walthall, Owen Moore, Kate Bruce.

THE RESTORATION—
CAST: Owen Moore, James Kirkwood, Marion Leonard.

THE LIGHT THAT CAME—
CAST: Marion Leonard, Kate Bruce, Mack Sennett, Arthur
Johnson, James Kirkwood, Joseph Graybill.

THE LITTLE TEACHER—
CAST: Arthur Johnson.

THE LONELY VILLA—
CAST: Marion Leonard.

IN THE WATCHES OF THE NIGHT—

1910: AS IT IS IN LIFE—
CAST: Gladys Eagen, Marion Leonard, Kate Bruce.

MUGGSY'S FIRST SWEETHEART—
CAST: Billy Quirk, Flora Finch.

An exciting scene from The Lonely Villa *(1909), Mary Pickford's first film appearance. Produced by Biograph studios, the film also starred Marion Leonard and Adele DeGarde.*

One of Mary's early films, The Test, *filmed in 1909.*

Mary Pickford and David Miles in The Violin Maker of Cremona, *1909.*

Billy Quirk with Mary in They Would Elope, *1909.*

Billy Quirk takes aim at Mary in The Hessian Renegades, *1909.*

85

Henry B. Walthall, Owen Moore, and Kate Bruce star with Mary in In Old
Kentucky Home, *1909.*

Demure Mary Pickford with Arthur Johnson in a scene from The Little
Teacher, *1909.*

Mary shares good news with James Kirkwood and Billy Quirk (Oh, Uncle!, 1909).

A violent reaction in Wilful Peggy, *starring Mary Pickford and Claire McDowell (1910).*

Mack Sennett and Mary in An Arcadian Maid, *1910.*

Ramona, *a love story with an unhappy ending, starring Mary, Henry B. Walthall, and Francis Grandin (1910).*

Mary seems totally helpless in another scene from An Arcadian Maid.

THE UNCHANGING SEA—
CAST: Linda Arvidson (Mrs. D. W. Griffith), Arthur Johnson.
WILFUL PEGGY—
CAST: Claire McDowell.
RAMONA—
CAST: Henry B. Walthall, Francis Grandin.
AN ARCADIAN MAID—
CAST: Mack Sennett.
WHITE ROSES—
CAST: Jack Pickford.
SONG OF THE WILDWOOD FLUTE—
1911: THREE SISTERS—
CAST: Vivian Prescott, Marion Sunshine, Mack Sennett.
A DECREE OF DESTINY—
CAST: Joseph Graybill, Marion Sunshine, Mack Sennett.
HOME FOLKS—
CAST: Robert Harron, Kate Bruce, Charles H. Mailes.
LENA AND THE GEESE—
Pickford wrote and starred in this story.

Mary Pickford with brother Jack in White Roses, *1910.*

Mary and Linda Arvidson (Mrs. D. W. Griffith) in The Unchanging Sea, *1910.*

90

Mary as an Indian girl in Song of the Wildwood Flute, *1910.*

A scene from Decree of Destiny, *1911.*

Pickford was then put under contract by Carl Laemmle, head of Universal "IMP" productions for whom she made 32 one-reelers. Only a few of these are still in existence. She then moved to Majestic and only one of her films made here remains. She returned to Biograph in 1912 and worked again under Griffith's supervision.

AT BIOGRAPH

1912: FATE'S INTERCEPTION—
    CAST: Wilfred Lucas.
    THE FEMALE OF THE SPECIES—
    CAST: Claire McDowell, Dorothy Bernard.
    THE OLD ACTOR—
    CAST: W. Chrystie, Charles West.
    THE NEW YORK HAT—
    CAST: Lionel Barrymore, Mae Marsh, Dorothy & Lillian Gish.
    JUST LIKE A WOMAN—
    CAST: Wilfred Lucas.
    THE ONE SHE LOVED—
    CAST: Lionel Barrymore.
    A PUEBLO LEGEND—a two reeler
    CAST: Wilfred Lucas, Robert Harron.
    FRIENDS—

Mary with Robert Harron, Kate Bruce, and Charles H. Mailes in Home Folks, *1911.*

Mary rounds up her geese in Lena and the Geese, *1911. Mary wrote the scenario for this film.*

Frowning Miss Pickford in Female of the Species, *1912.*

Mary sheds a look of dismay in this tender scene from The One She Loved, *1912, with Lionel Barrymore.*

Mary is surrounded by Lionel Barrymore and Charles Mailes in The New York Hat, *1912.*

Lionel Barrymore and Mary Pickford in another scene from The New York Hat.

CAST: Lionel Barrymore, H. B. Walthall, Harry Carey, Charles H. Mailes, Robert Harron.

SO NEAR, YET SO FAR—

CAST: Robert Harron, Elmer Booth, Walter Miller, Lionel Barrymore, Antonio Moreno.

MY BABY—

CAST: Henry B. Walthall, W. Chrystie Miller, Lionel Barrymore.

THE INFORMER—

CAST: H. B. Walthall, Walter Miller, Kate Bruce, Lionel Barrymore.

1913: THE UNWELCOME GUEST—

CAST: W. Chrystie Miller, Claire McDowell, Charles H. Mailes, Elmer Booth, Jack Pickford, Lillian Gish, Harry Carey.

AT FAMOUS PLAYERS AND ARTCRAFT (PARAMOUNT)

1913: IN THE BISHOP'S CARRIAGE—directed by Edwin S. Porter & J. Searle Dawley, Camera: Edwin S. Porter.

CAST: David V. Wall, House Peters.

CAPRICE—directed by J. Searle Dawley.

A scene from Friends, *1912.*

Mary repairs torn net in Mender of Nets, *1912.*

Just Like a Woman, *with Mary and Wilfred Lucas (1912).*

Mary fixes her hair admiringly in a scene from In the Bishop's Carriage, *1913.*   **97**

Mary as Mercy decides to wear the old gingham gown in Caprice, *1913. Louise Huff looks on.*

CAST: Ernest Truex, Owen Moore, Louise Huff, Howard Missimer.

1914: HEART'S ADRIFT—directed by Edwin S. Porter. Camera: Edwin S. Porter.

CAST: Harold Lockwood.

A GOOD LITTLE DEVIL—directed by Edwin S. Porter. Camera: Edwin S. Porter.

CAST: Ernest Truex, William Norris, Edward Connelly.

TESS OF THE STORM COUNTRY—directed by Edwin S. Porter. Camera: Edwin S. Porter.

CAST: David Hartford, Olive Fuller Golden, Harold Lockwood.

THE EAGLE'S MATE—directed by James Kirkwood.

CAST: James Kirkwood, Ida Waterman.

SUCH A LITTLE QUEEN—Directed by Hugh Ford.

CAST: Carlyle Blackwell, Russell Bassett, Arthur Hoops, Harold Lockwood.

BEHIND THE SCENES—Directed by James Kirkwood.

Mary in a scene from Caprice.

CAST: James Kirkwood, Lowell Sherman, Ida Waterman, Russell Bassett.

CINDERELLA—Directed by James Kirkwood.

CAST: Owen Moore, Georgia Wilson.

1915: MISTRESS NELL—Directed by James Kirkwood.

CAST: Owen Moore, Arthur Hoops, Ruby Hoffman.

FANCHON THE CRICKET—Directed by James Kirkwood.

Mercy attempts suicide with a bulletless gun in Caprice, *directed by J. Searle Dawly.*

"Father, take me back to the old home!" Mary and Howard Missimer in Caprice.

Heart's Adrift, *directed by Edwin S. Porter, starred Mary Pickford and Harold Lockwood. Here, Mary is frightened by the lightning.*

Mary defends herself against Harold Lockwood in Heart's Adrift, *1914.*

The deserted couple repeat the lines of the marriage ceremony together (Heart's Adrift).

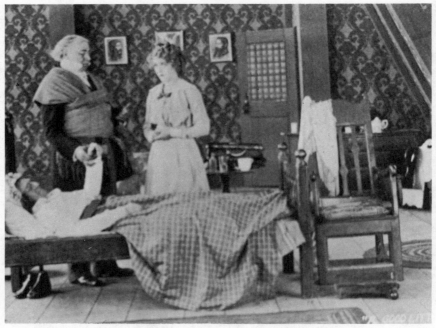

Mary and William Norris in A Good Little Devil, *1914.*

King and Queen of fairy realms (A Good Little Devil).

Mary Pickford as Tess tries to comfort Harold Lockwood in Tess of the Storm Country, *1914.*

103

Fear on Mary's face and a looming shadow in the background are evidence of an uninvited guest (Tess of the Storm Country).

Jean Hersholt and Mary in a scene from Tess of the Storm Country.

Cinderella, *directed by James Kirkwood, starred Mary Pickford, Owen Moore, and Georgia Wilson (1914).*

Mary rides along with a group of men in The Eagle's Mate, *1914, also starring James Kirkwood and Ida Waterman.*

Mary holds the betrothal cup in Such a Little Queen, *directed by Hugh Ford and also starring Carlyle Blackwell (1914).*

James Kirkwood assures Mary (Dolly) that tomorrow he is going to look for a little flat for two (Behind the Scenes, 1914).

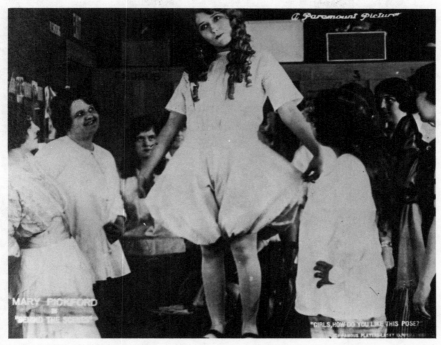

Mary demonstrates to her girlfriends an unusual pose in Behind the Scenes.

CAST: Jack and Lottie Pickford, Gertrude Norman, Jack Standing, Fred and Adele Astaire.

THE DAWN OF TOMORROW—Directed by James Kirkwood.

CAST: David Powell, Forest Robinson, Robert Cain.

LITTLE PAL—Directed by James Kirkwood.

CAST: Russell Bassett, George Anderson.

RAGS—Directed by James Kirkwood.

CAST: Marshall Neilan, Joseph Manning, J. Farrell MacDonald.

ESMERALDA—Directed by James Kirkwood.

CAST: Ida Waterman, Fuller Mellish, Arthur Hoops, Charles Waldron.

A GIRL OF YESTERDAY—Directed by Allan Dwan.

CAST: Gertrude Norman, Frances Marion, Jack Pickford, Donald Crisp, Marshall Neilan, Glenn Martin.

MADAME BUTTERFLY—directed by Sidney Olcott. Camera: Hal Young.

A scene from Dawn of a Tomorrow, *1915.*

Sir Oliver sees a new phase of life in Dawn of a Tomorrow.

108

Mary Pickford and Owen Moore as lovers in Mistress Nell, *1915.*

*Mary cannot believe that David is dead. Ida Waterman watches as she receives the bad news (*Esmeralda, *1915).*

Couple announce their love for each other to Ida Waterman in Esmeralda, *1915.*

Mary is sad when she thinks of leaving the old home (Esmeralda).

Poor fatherless, motherless "Rags." Also starring with Mary Pickford in Rags *(1915) were Marshall Neilan, Joseph Manning and J. Farrell MacDonald.*

J. Farrell MacDonald accuses Marshall Neilan of sneaking in to see "Rags."

111

Mary in a scene from Rags.

"No place to go but out, and no place to come but back." Mary in Rags.

Mary dances with Glenn Martin in The Girl of Yesterday, *1915. Frances Marion and Marshall Neilan at right.*

Mary Pickford and Marshall Neilan in a touching scene from Madame Butterfly *(1915)—the beginning of the romance between Cho-Cho-San and Lieut. Pinkerton.*

Mary seems tired and disgusted in this scene from The Eternal Grind, *1916.*

Mary with Maggie Weston and Mildred Morris in The Foundling, *1916.*

Mary stuffs her hands and pockets with fruit in Poor Little Pepina, *1916.*

CAST: Marshall Neilan, W. T. Carleton, Olive West, Caroline Harris, Cesare Gravina.

1916: THE FOUNDLING—Directed by John B. O'Brien. Camera: H. J. Siddons.

CAST: Edward Martindel, Maggie Weston, Mildred Morris, Marcia Harris.

POOR LITTLE PEPPINA—Directed by Sidney Olcott.

CAST: Eugene O'Brien, Edwin Mordant, Edith Shayne, Cesare Gravina, Jack Pickford, W. T. Carleton.

Mary Pickford and David Powell in Less than the Dust, *1916.*

Hulda (Mary Pickford) and her three little brothers start for America in a scene from Hulda from Holland, *1916.*

Getting ready for the trip to the promised land (Hulda from Holland).

Hulda and her three brothers arrive in America.

Matt Moore gives Mary a peace offering in The Pride of the Clan, *1917.*

Marget (Mary Pickford) and Jamie (Matt Moore) are together in The Pride of the Clan.

THE ETERNAL GRIND—Directed by John B. O'Brien.

CAST: John Bowers, Robert Cain, Loretta Blake, Dorothy West.

HULDA FROM HOLLAND—Directed by John B. O'Brien.

CAST: John Bowers, Frank Losee, Russell Bassett.

LESS THAN THE DUST—Directed by John Emerson. Camera: George Hill.

CAST: David Powell, Mary Alden, Cesare Gravina, Russell Bassett.

1917: THE PRIDE OF THE CLAN—Directed by Maurice Tourneur. Camera: Lucien Andriot.

CAST: Matt Moore, Kathryn Browne Decker, Warren Cook.

THE POOR LITTLE RICH GIRL—directed by Maurice Tourneur. Camera: John Van Der Broeck, Lucien Andriot.

CAST: Madlaine Traverse, Charles Wellesly, Gladys Fairbanks, Frank McGlyn, Herbert Prior, Marcia Harris.

ROMANCE OF THE REDWOODS—Directed by Cecil B. DeMille. Camera: Alvin Wyckoff.

Mary Pickford gets a scolding in a scene from Poor Little Rich Girl, *1917.*

119

Marcia Harris tells the "poor little rich girl" that her mother is too busy to see her.

CAST: Elliott Dexter, Charles Ogle, Tully Marshall, Raymond Hatton.

THE LITTLE AMERICAN—Directed by Cecil B. DeMille. Camera: Alvin Wyckoff.

CAST: Jack Holt, Hobart Bosworth, James Neil, Guy Oliver, Ben Alexander, Walter Long, Raymond Hatton, Ramon Novarro (extra).

REBECCA OF SUNNYBROOK FARM—Directed by Marshall Neilan. Camera: Walter Stradling.

CAST: Eugene O'Brien, Helen Jerome Eddy, Charles Ogle, Marjorie Daw, Josephine Crowell, Wesley Barry.

A LITTLE PRINCESS—Directed by Marshall Neilan. Camera: Walter Stradling, Charles Rosher.

CAST: Norman Kerry, Zasu Pitts, Katherine Griffith, Anne Schaefer, Theodore Roberts, Gertrude Short, Gustav von Seyffertitz.

STELLA MARIS—Directed by Marshall Neilan. Camera: Walter Stradling.

To her maid's dismay, Mary makes a mess (Poor Little Rich Girl).

CAST: Conway Tearle, Camille Ankewich (Marcia Mannon), Ida Waterman, Josephine Crowell.

AMARILLY OF CLOTHES-LINE ALLEY—Directed by Marshall Neilan. Camera: Walter Stradling.

CAST: Norman Kerry, Herbert Standing, William Scott, Ida Waterman, Wesley Barry, Kate Price.

M'LISS—Directed by Marshall Neilan. Camera: Walter Stradling.

CAST: Theodore Roberts, Thomas Meighan, Tully Marshall, Charles Ogle, Monte Blue.

HOW COULD YOU, JEAN?—Directed by William Desmond Taylor. Camera: Charles Rosher.

CAST: Casson Ferguson, Herbert Standing, Spottiswoode Aitken, Zazu Pitts.

JOHANNA ENLISTS—Directed by William Desmond Taylor. Camera: Charles Rosher.

CAST: Anne Schaefer, Fred Huntley, Monte Blue, Douglas MacLean, Emory Johnson, Wallace Beery.

Mary Pickford, an accomplished producer as well as star, is seen here with her toys, appearing to be quite bored, in a scene from Poor Little Rich Girl.

THE SWEETHEARTS FACE DEATH TOGETHER

MARY PICKFORD IN "THE LITTLE AMERICAN"

The sweethearts, Mary Pickford and Jack Holt, face death together in The Little American.

122

Mary Pickford in Romance of the Redwoods, *directed by Cecil B. De Mille in 1917.*

Mary Pickford and Walter Long in a scene from The Little American, *directed by De Mille in 1917.*

On board the torpedoed Vertania (The Little American).

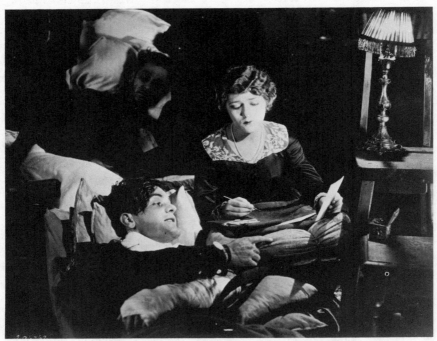

Mary Pickford with Ramon Novarro in The Little American.

124

Angela baffles the enemy in The Little American.

Rebecca (Mary) at home with the little children (Rebecca of Sunnybrook Farm, 1917).

Rebecca is the queen of the circus. Wesley Barry and Charles Ogle look on.

Charles Ogle removes the stains of travel from Rebecca's face in Rebecca of Sunnybrook Farm.

Mary Pickford with Josephine Crowell, Eugene O'Brien, and Mayme Kelso in a scene from Rebecca of Sunnybrook Farm.

Mary reclines in style in The Little Princess.

Mary Pickford discovers something new in a scene from The Little Princess, *directed by Marshall Neilan in 1917.*

1919: CAPTAIN KIDD JR—Directed by William Desmond Taylor. Camera: Charles Rosher.
>
> CAST: Douglas MacLean, Robert Gordon, Spottiswoode Aitken.

AT FIRST NATIONAL
> DADDY LONG LEGS—Directed by Marshall Neilan. Camera: Charles Rosher & Henry Cronjager.
>
> CAST: Mahlon Hamilton, Marshall Neilan, Wesley Barry.

128

Mary finds the situation a little "hair-raising" in The Little Princess.

Mary Pickford in Stella Maris, *directed by Marshall Neilan in 1917.*

Mary Pickford and Conway Tearle in Stella Maris.

THE HOODLUM—Directed by Sidney Franklin. Camera: Charles Rosher.

CAST: Kenneth Harlan, Max Davidson, Dwight Crittenden, Andrew Arbuckle, Ralph Lewis, Buddie Messenger.

HEART O'THE HILLS—Directed by Sidney Franklin. Camera: Charles Rosher.

CAST: John Gilbert, Sam De Grasse, Claire McDowell.

130

Stella's kind words deeply touched Unity Blake. Mary Pickford as Unity Blake (left) and Stella Maris (right).

The bottle—the origin of all her woes and her semi-insanity. Mary Pickford and Marcia Mannon in a scene from Stella Maris.

131

Mary Pickford with Ida Waterman and Conway Tearle in Stella Maris.

Herbert Standing and Mary Pickford in a scene from Amarilly of Clothes-Line Alley *(1917)*.

Mary Pickford in Amarilly of Clothes-Line Alley.

Mary sweeps up in Amarilly of Clothes-Line Alley.

The morning after the night before. Norman Kerry and Kate Price with Mary Pickford in this scene from Amarilly of Clothes-Line Alley.

Theodore Roberts and Mary in M'Liss, *1917.*

Theodore Roberts, Charles Ogle, and Mary in a scene from M'Liss.

Mary and Theodore Roberts examine the tail feathers of Hildegarde in M'Liss.

Mary catches Wesley Barry with the goods in How Could You Jean? *(1917).*

Mary Pickford discovers that Casson Ferguson is a miserable fraud (How Could You Jean?).

Mary as Johanna tests the stew in Johanna Enlists, *1917.*

Mary speaks with Douglas MacLean in Johanna Enlists.

Mary Pickford with Anne Schaefer and Emory Johnson in Johanna Enlists.

Mary is courted in Johanna Enlists.

138

Mary Pickford consults Polly where the treasure might be buried in Captain Kidd, Jr., *1919.*

Marcia Mannon, Spottiswoode Aitken, Doug MacLean and Mary in a scene from Captain Kidd, Jr.

139

Mary Pickford with Douglas MacLean in Captain Kidd, Jr.

Mary comforts her grandfather (Spottiswoode Aitken), as her husband, Jim (Douglas MacLean), looks on (Captain Kidd, Jr.).

Mahlon Hamilton and Mary Pickford in Daddy Long Legs, *1919.*

A picnic for three—Marshall Neilan, Mary Pickford, and Mahlon Hamilton— in Daddy Long Legs.

Mary is surrounded by children in Daddy Long Legs.

Mary gets involved in a fight in Heart O'The Hills, *1919.*

Mary in a scene from Heart O'The Hills.

143

Mary and her trusty rifle pose on a donkey in Heart O'The Hills.

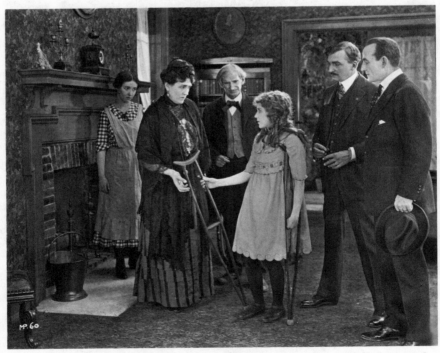

Mary Pickford sheds her crutches in Pollyanna, 1920. *Looking on are Helen Jerome Eddy, Katherine Griffith, J. Warton James, Herbert Prior, and George Barrell.*

Mary is dressed as a comical character in Suds, *1920.*

AT UNITED ARTISTS

1920: POLLYANNA—Directed by Paul Powell. Camera: Charles
Rosher.
    CAST: William Courtleigh, Helen Jerome Eddy, Herbert Prior,
        Doc Crane, Mrs. Griffith.
    SUDS—Directed by Jack Dillon. Camera: Charles Rosher.
    CAST: William Austin, Theodore Roberts, Harold Goodwin.

The dream sequence from Suds, *directed by John F. Dillon.*

1921: THE LOVE LIGHT—Directed by Frances Marion. Camera: Charles Rosher, Henry Cronjager.
CAST: Fred Thomson, Evelyn Duma, Raymond Bloomer.
THROUGH THE BACK DOOR—Directed by Alfred E. Green & Jack Pickford. Camera: Charles Rosher.
CAST: John Harron, Adolph Menjou, Peaches Jackson, Gertrude Astor, Elinor Fair, Wilfred Lucas.
LITTLE LORD FAUNTLEROY—Directed by Alfred E.

146

Mary has something secret to tell (Pollyanna).

Mary Pickford and Fred Thomson play games in a scene from The Love Light, *1921.*

Mary Pickford and Fred Thomson have a disagreement in The Love Light.

Mary exhibits a bit of love for animals in this scene from Through the Back Door, *1921.*

148

Mary fixes her shoe in Through the Back Door, *which was co-directed by her brother Jack and Alfred E. Green.*

Mary does her chores in Through the Back Door.

149

Mary, as Little Lord Fauntleroy, poses with the village children (Little Lord Fauntleroy, *1921*).

Fauntleroy gives a clever impersonation of his grandfather, the Earl. The Reverend Mordaunt is played by Emmett King.

150

Green & Jack Pickford. Camera: Charles Rosher.
Mary played the Little Lord and his mother in a dual role.
CAST: Claude Gillingwater, Kate Price.

1922: TESS OF THE STORM COUNTRY—Directed by John S. Robertson. Camera: Charles Rosher.
CAST: Lloyd Hughes, Gloria Hope, Jean Hersholt.
(Her only Film Remake.)

1923: ROSITA—Directed by Ernst Lubitsch. Camera: Charles Rosher.
CAST: George Walsh, Holbrook Blinn, Irene Rich, George Periolat.

1924: DOROTHY VERNON OF HADDON HALL—Directed by Marshall Neilan. Camera: Charles Rosher.
CAST: Allan Forest, Clare Eames, Lottie Pickford, Marc Mac-Dermott, Estelle Taylor, Anders Randolf.

1925: LITTLE ANNIE ROONEY—Directed by William Beaudine. Camera: Charles Rosher, Hal Mohr.
CAST: William Haines, Gordon Griffith, Carlo Schipa, Vola Vale.

Fauntleroy with Claude Gillingwater.

Mary reads her bible in an improvised bed in the second version of Tess of the Storm Country, *directed by John S. Robertson (1922).*

Mary is rejected and downtrodden in a lonely scene from Rosita, *1923.*

Mary Pickford and children in Rosita.

Holbrook Blinn and Mary in Rosita.

153

Mary and Spanish family in Rosita.

Mary Pickford points an accusing finger that wins Queen Elizabeth's (Clare Eames's) attention in Dorothy Vernon of Haddon Hall, *1924.*

Mary Pickford casts a doubtful glance in Dorothy Vernon of Haddon Hall.

Mary with Anders Randolph, Marc MacDermott, and Alan Forest (Dorothy Vernon of Haddon Hall).

155

Devilish Annie is played by Mary Pickford in Little Annie Rooney, *1925.*

Mary Pickford as Little Annie Rooney.

Mary scolds kids in Little Annie Rooney.

Annie Rooney receives a message by way of a doll.

Mary makes a discovery as children look on (Sparrows).

1926: SPARROWS—Directed by William Beaudine. Camera: Charles Rosher, Karl Struss, Hal Mohr.

CAST: Roy Stewart, Mary Louise Miller, Gustav von Seffertitz. (This feature teamed with Douglas Fairbanks' BLACK PIRATE premiered at Grauman's Egyptian Theatre in Hollywood.)

158

Mary and children fear the interloper in Sparrows, *1926.*

Children get washed (Sparrows).

Mary Pickford and Charles "Buddy" Rogers in My Best Girl, *1927.*

Mary finds herself in a predicament in My Best Girl.

Buddy Rogers and Mary enjoy dinner for two (My Best Girl).

The lovers (Pickford and Rogers) share an umbrella in My Best Girl.

1927: MY BEST GIRL—Directed by Sam Taylor. Camera: Charles
    Rosher.
    CAST: Charles "Buddy" Rogers, Hobart Bosworth, Mack
        Swain, Lucien Littlefield.
    THE GAUCHO—Directed by F. Richard Jones.
    CAST: Douglas Fairbanks, Lupe Velez, Eve Southern. Pickford
        appeared as THE MADONNA.

Johnny Mack Brown holds Mary Pickford in Coquette, 1929, *directed by Sam Taylor. Mary won the first talkie Oscar for her performance.*

1929: COQUETTE—Directed by Sam Taylor. Camera: Karl Struss.
CAST: John Mack Brown, George Irving, Louise Beavers, Matt Moore, William Janney, John St. Polis. (Pickford won the first talkie Oscar for her performance.)
THE TAMING OF THE SHREW—Directed by Sam Taylor —additional dialogue by Sam Taylor from Shakespeare's play. Camera: Karl Struss.

Mary, Johnny Mack Brown, and John St. Polis in Coquette.

CAST: Douglas Fairbanks, Edwin Maxwell, Joseph Cawthorn, Clyde Cook, Geoffrey Wardswell, Dorothy Jordan.

1931: KIKI—Directed by Sam Taylor. Camera: Karl Struss.

CAST: Reginald Denny, Margaret Livingston, Joseph Cawthorn.

1933: SECRETS—Directed by Frank Borzage. Camera: Ray June.

CAST: Leslie Howard, C. Aubrey Smith, Blanche Frederici, Ned Sparks, Ethel Clayton, Bessie Barriscale.

Mary Pickford in Taming of the Shrew, *1929*.

Mary Pickford and Douglas Fairbanks in a scene from Taming of the Shrew.

Mary looking elegant and Doug looking disheveled in Taming of the Shrew.

Mary prepares for Fairbanks's offering (Taming of the Shrew).

Mary comforts her husband in Taming of the Shrew.

168

Mary Pickford and cast in a dancing scene from Kiki, *1931.*

Mary strikes a flirtatious pose in Kiki.

Mary Pickford and Reginald Denny in Kiki.

Mary Pickford with Reginald Denny in Kiki.

A tender scene with Leslie Howard and Mary Pickford from Secrets, *1933.*

172

Doris Lloyd and Mary Pickford in Secrets.

Mary is dressed in an exquisite gown in Secrets.

Mary Pickford with Leslie Howard, Doris Lloyd, and Blanche Frederici (Se-crets).

Mary is interrupted while feeding the baby (Secrets).

Fearful Mary holds on to Leslie Howard (Secrets).